Date Due

HEN Oct 83			
JAN 1 9			
MAY 1 1984			
MAY 3 0 1985			
AUG 2 9 1985			
NOV 2 4 1987			
DEC 3 1987			
SEP 2 5 1990			

ALBERTA
A Symphony in Colour

Text by Ted Ferguson

Collins Toronto

The valley appears without warning. After a hundred miles of rolling, crop-heavy fields, the land suddenly gives way to a vast, desolate hollow, 500 feet below the prairie surface. Cacti, rattlesnakes and sagebrush flourish amongst the clay and sandstone formations where, on cloudless summer days, the temperature can soar to 130°F.

A tall, young paleontologist, Philip Currie, stands on a windy ridge deep in the Badlands valley and watches a female volunteer lift a thick bone from a carefully-dug hole. It is a shoulder bone from a Centrosaurus dinosaur that was destroyed by a flash flood 70 million years ago.

"This is really exciting work," Currie says, kneeling to study the bronze fossil. "You can almost feel yourself jump back in time. As far as I'm concerned, having a strong sense of history is important to every human being."

Most other Albertans would agree. For the past two decades, since it was blessed with a burst of unprecedented prosperity, the province has been passionately committed to a profound and affectionate examination of

The Alaska Highway these pages runs from Fairbanks in the State of Alaska to "Mile-O" at Dawson Creek in B.C. The drive has been called the experience of a lifetime, and it is easy to see why. Much of the road is narrow, winding, and very dusty – and the dust manages to find its way everywhere! Despite broad daylight, it is necessary to drive with headlights on to see through the dust . . . Both headlights and windscreens get broken, and the driver is frequently subjected to "freeze-ups" or "washouts." This may sound like a nightmare, but the Alaska Highway is, almost always, referred to with affection by the drivers who tackle it regularly.

its historical roots. Impressive museums and re-constructed forts draw thousands of visitors annually; books of local history are regional best-sellers; the educational TV network, ACCESS, reports an increased viewership whenever historical documentaries are aired. While the Age of the Dinosaur is an extremely popular topic, the majority of Albertans have shown a greater interest in two more recent subjects – the era of the frontier cowboy and the pioneering farmers' gritty resolve to inhabit a hostile land.

Neither the cowboys nor the farmers were, however, the province's first white settlers. That distinction belongs to the fur traders. In 1754, Anthony Henday crossed the Prairies by foot and horse and set up camp at a spot on the ice-clogged North Saskatchewan River that eventually became the capital city, Edmonton. Henday explored the area for seven weeks, exchanging blankets and tools for beaver pelts. In his wake came a swarm of Hudson's Bay and North West Company traders and, by 1800, both companies had peppered the northern region with trading posts.

The rivalry between the Hudson's Bay men and the Nor'westers was intense. They often built posts within sight of each other so they could keep track of their competitors' business dealings: if one post seemed to be doing better than the other, an overnight robbery or a suspicious fire would sometimes tip the balance back.

By the mid-1800s, there were 40 competing posts throughout Alberta. As rowdy as many of them were, none could match an independent operation for sheer wantonness. Bearing a very suitable name, Fort Whoop-Up was the scene of what might be termed a continuous wild party. Founded in 1869 by two disreputable Americans, Joe Healy and Alf Hamilton, Whoop-Up specialized in the swapping of rot-gut whisky for buffalo hides and other smaller pelts. There were no lawmen at the fort, a fact that drew many notorious outlaws across the Montana Territory border, 60 miles south. When they weren't shooting one another during drunken brawls, they were killing Indians: one summer alone, 88 Blackfoot were slain within the stockade's crudely-made log walls. The Hudson's Bay Company vigorously urged the federal government to do something about Fort Whoop-Up but its pleas were ignored.

Then came the Cypress Hills Massacre. In May, 1873, a 29-year-old Missouri native, Tom Hardwicke, was returning to Montana with 13 other wolf hunters after spending the winter around Fort Calgary. Some of their horses disappeared overnight and, assuming Indians had stolen them, Hardwicke led his party into the Cypress Hills west of Fort Whoop-Up. Encountering an Assiniboine band, Hardwicke accused them of taking the animals. An argument broke out and, opening fire with repeater rifles, the hunters killed over 30 men, women and children.

Reports of the massacre enraged Prime Minister John A. Macdonald. He bulldozed a bill through Parliament creating the North West Mounted Police and,

Edmonton left is the capital of Alberta and also the most northerly of Canada's major cities. Overleaf can be seen a spectacular night view of the Legislative Buildings.

The capital of Alberta is Edmonton these pages, a city with a population of over half a million. Downtown Edmonton left has a seemingly ever-changing skyline as new buildings grow skywards. The Provincial Museum opposite page below was completed in 1967 to coincide with, and commemorate, Canada's Centennial Year. The history of Alberta is laid out in the museum, exhibits including displays of early Indian life and pioneer settlement as well as geology and natural history. Ultramodern architecture characterizes parts of Edmonton, as seen beside the Court House opposite page top, while overleaf can be seen the glittering skyline of the city revealed by nightfall.

the following spring, a red-jacketed detachment of 275 men trekked west. Hardwicke and others involved in the massacre fled to the United States and, although the killers escaped justice, the Mounties quickly succeeded in their primary goal, bringing law and order to Fort Whoop-Up.

The Mounties not only tamed Whoop-Up but they are generally credited with keeping the Canadian Old West considerably less violent than its American counterpart. There were no legend-shrouded gunslingers like Billy the Kid, no mob lynchings similar to the Ox Bow Incident, and not a single Mountie died in a High Noon-style battle. Nevertheless, the cattle-ranching industry that began on the southern Alberta plains in the mid-1800s did attract a varied mixture of cardsharps, prostitutes, rustlers, Bible-thumpers, bandits and general all-round characters to the shanty towns that replaced the log forts.

John George 'Kootenai' Brown was, by anybody's standard, the greatest frontiersman of the lot. A lanky Irishman who could quote Shakespeare and Tennyson, Brown arrived in Canada in 1864, abandoning a British Army career where, it was said, he had killed a fellow officer in a duel. Despite his quiet, gentlemanly manner, he adapted swiftly to the rough frontier life and, among other things, he became a prospector, muleskinner, peace officer, pony express rider, buffalo hunter and military scout. He survived at least two brushes with marauding Indians. Hit by an arrow at an Alberta watering hole, he killed two braves before pouring turpentine in the wound and riding 20 miles to safety. On another occasion, Brown was taken prisoner by Sitting Bull and a Sioux war party when he was carrying mail across the Dakota Territory: he escaped by rolling down an embankment while the Sioux were preparing a fire to roast him, and walking 50 miles, naked and sun-blistered, to an army post.

Like Brown, the cowboys working on the ranches sometimes clashed violently with the Indians but their main problems were caused by other whites. Rustling gangs roamed the prairies and highwaymen waylaid them on lonely trails. Rancher Bill Mitchell took matters into his own hands when the Bears' Paw Gang stole his horses. He rode to the ringleaders' cabin unarmed and, kicking the door open, announced, "I've come for my animals." The gang members were so awed by his courage that they surrendered the animals without an argument.

As if dealing with outlaws wasn't tough enough, cattlemen had to cope with life in the frontier towns when they had time off. Gamblers prowled the saloons and the performers included the likes of Little Lou, an overweight singer and part-time muleskinner. The saloons and brothels provided the cowhands with a full plate of local gossip. It was in those tawdry establishments that they would hear how cardsharp Billy Morton auctioned off the woman he won in a poker game or how John Ware, a black cowboy, defied a local edict by taking a shortcut through downtown Calgary – driving several hundred steers in front of him.

The coming of the railway, electricity, the telephone and, perhaps the most influential force of all, religious reform movements, introduced a new form of civilization to the West. So did the arrival of the immigrants: in the late 1800s, Interior Minister Clifford Sifton masterminded the biggest land giveaway in the country's history. Enticed by the promise of 160 free acres, two million newcomers emigrated to Canada by 1911. One third came from the British Isles, another third from the United States and the remaining third from central Europe.

Many Westerners hotly opposed the importation of the central Europeans, especially the lower-class Ukrainians, because they wanted Canada to be solidly Anglo-Saxon. Sifton was steadfast. In an oft-quoted speech, he stated:

"I think a stalwart peasant in a sheepskin coat, born on the soil, whose forebearers have been farmers for ten

generations, with a stout wife and a half dozen children, good quality. They ask for nothing more than land and a chance to work. The man who works hard usually makes good and values his success."

Two hundred thousand Ukrainians flocked to Canada and the majority put down roots on the Prairies. The hard work that Sifton referred to was carried out under dreadful living conditions. What little cash the newcomers possessed often went to buy a horse and plow: many Ukrainian families around Edmonton inhabited sod huts and a group of Icelanders spent their first winter near Calgary in caves dug into hillsides.

Women toiled as energetically as men, clearing trees and rocks and helping plant crops. On frigid winter nights, huddled beside wood-burning stoves, wives wove cotton and wool for clothing and, if their husbands took summer jobs in treacherous coal mines or logging camps to earn sorely-needed money, they suffered from anxiety and loneliness.

Roughly one half of the immigrants left Alberta within a few years of their arrival. Those who stayed and endured made slow progress. And just when all of the deprivation had ended for some settlers – and they could at last begin to enjoy life – the Great Depression all but

To be found in the city of Edmonton are the Citadel Theater right and the Muttart Conservatory left, above and overleaf. Within each pyramid at the conservatory, which was opened in 1976, is a carefully controlled environment, reproducing the climate and flora of a given location.

wiped out their gains. Second-generation farmers, many harboring memories of grim childhoods, found themselves facing financial hardship in the 1930s. It was not unique to come across a Dust Bowl farmer trading his favorite horse for sacks of flour while his son shot a prairie chicken for dinner and his wife patched shirts and trousers she'd have used for rags in better times.

World War II saw a marked increase in the demand for grain but it wasn't until after the fighting ceased that the economic picture really brightened. In the decade between 1946 and 1956 Canada's gross national product doubled. Although farming and coal-mining played prominent roles, the province owed most of its newborn affluence to the aftermath of an auspicious event that occurred on a snow-steeped field outside Edmonton on February 13, 1947.

At 10.00 a.m. that day, a dozen Imperial Oil executives and a few reporters gathered around an antiquated drill rig on Mike Turta's farm near the town of Leduc. Tests had shown there were extensive oil and gas deposits 5,000 feet

beneath the rig and the nattily-dressed dignitaries had converged on the site to watch a denim-clad crew start the supposedly easy pumping operation.

The rig had been in service for almost 30 years, drilling 133 holes and not striking anything worth recovering until two weeks earlier at Leduc. The onlookers were in for a long wait. The rig had broken a shaft during an early-morning trial run. The crew labored feverishly to repair the damage and, shortly after 4.00 p.m., oil and gas finally rushed up the line. The executives applauded, the reporters scribbled notes, the crew breathed a collective sigh of relief. Site boss Vern Hunter later recalled that the crew knew they had brought in a good well yet no one even suspected they were sparking a truly significant event, the transformation of Alberta's floundering petroleum business into a major North American industry.

Paced by the Leduc field (which has, to date, yielded an awesome 355 million barrels), the Alberta production rate leapt from 18,000 barrels a day in 1946 to 75,000 a day in

Calgary these pages and overleaf lies where the Bow and Elbow rivers meet and the name "Calgary" is Gaelic for "clear running water." The modern skyline is dominated by the Calgary Tower, featured in these photographs. The tower reaches a height of 620 feet, and houses an observation deck and a revolving restaurant.

1950. A Belgian company, Petrofina, was the first foreign firm to create an Alberta subsidiary during the fifties; Shell Canada Limited, which had decided to shut down its unsuccessful exploration division, reversed its stand following the Leduc strike.

New discoveries were made throughout the province over the next three decades, including the Pembina field that proved to be even more productive than Leduc. Pipelines and refineries were built and, in the 1960s, the province experienced a population boom. The oil industry helped change the character of Alberta's largest cities, Edmonton and Calgary. The slow-paced, rather insular communities became vibrant, cosmopolitan centers. At the same time, the post-war affluence

sweeping Europe and other parts of the world was fated to have a substantial impact on a drowsy mountain settlement named after a Scottish community known for its fine whisky. The town was Banff.

The Rockies

It is easy to understand why the Rocky Mountains are Alberta's No. 1 tourist lure. The towering limestone peaks are laced with wooded valleys, flower-bunched meadows, cascading waterfalls and glistening white glaciers. Without leaving their vehicles, visitors have a chance to see deer, bighorn sheep, moose, mountain goats and, on occasion, the monarch of the wilderness, the grizzly.

Calgary is vibrant with life and energy – these being epitomized by the Calgary Stampede these and the following pages, a spectacular event held annually. The city has blossomed and grown over the last hundred years, and although it is in all senses a modern city, here the old west lives on. When the railroad was built it brought merchants and missionaries, ranchers and farmers, remittance men and, inevitably, a few scoundrels! Sarcee, Blood, Blackfoot, Stony and Piegan Indians came to trade here, and great herds of cattle were brought from the overgrazed ranches south of the border, to feed on the lush "short grass" which is so perfectly suited to raising prime beef animals.

CPR builder William Van Horne was among the first to recognize the Rockies' tourism potential. Upon viewing the mountains for the first time in the 1880s, the bombastic railroader declared, "We can't export the scenery. We'll import the tourists." At Van Horne's urging, the CPR erected a magnificent Scottish-style hotel, the Banff Springs, near a hot springs pool at the foot of Sulphur Mountain. When he looked at the blueprints one day – and realized that the kitchen faced the spectacular panoramic view – Van Horne immediately sketched a plan for a large, backyard rotunda to accommodate the guests.

The hotel drew a steady flow of middle and upper-class clientele from around the world. The original 250-room wooden structure was replaced by a 525-room limestone building in the 1920s. The hotel and hot springs have become an even bigger tourist attraction since the early 1960s. "Things used to be pretty quiet around Banff," says former chief park warden Andy Anderson. "Bighorn would wander the streets, black bears would forage in alley garbage cans. Before the tourist explosion happened, you could practically have driven a bus down the sidewalk on Banff Avenue on Saturday night without knocking anyone over."

Nowadays, an estimated five million people descend on the once-sleepy town every year. Most turn up during the summer and, on a warm August day, vehicles creep bumper-to-bumper along Banff Avenue. The sidewalks are also jammed: smart shops offer costly clothing, restaurants feature four-star dining and, with a large proportion of the visitors now coming from Japan, signs are sometimes written in English and Japanese.

Banff itself may be crowded but it is still possible to find a tranquil spot within a few miles of the town. The 2,500-square-mile Banff National Park encompasses 800 miles of bush trails. Hikers can go on day trips to one of the many lakes in the area or climb the slopes of the less precipitous mountains; some visitors take week-long trail rides through the passes under the guidance of experienced outfitters – a local tradition since Van Horne's time.

A Calgary tourist brochure eloquently describes the Calgary Stampede these pages in the following words: "The Greatest Dad-Burned Outdoor Show on Earth, held annually early in July. Ten days of western fun and excitement, ushered in by the spectacular Stampede parade, chuckwagon breakfasts . . . square dancing in the streets . . . parades of Mounties and Indians, cowboys, and pioneers each morning . . . world championship rodeo . . . chuckwagon races . . . dazzling stage shows with star celebrities . . . gambling casinos . . . nightclubs with entertainment from mild to wild. Don't just come to watch – come to participate!!"

Yes, for ten days every July, Calgary lives it up. Flapjacks and coffee, grandstand shows and fireworks, livestock exhibits, a huge funfair, and a village with Stony, Sarcee, Blood and Blackfoot Indians. Cowboys from all over Canada and the United States compete in the rodeo for prize-money amounting to over a quarter of a million dollars! And daily events include saddle and bareback bronco busting, Brahma bull and buffalo riding, a wild-horse race, steer wrestling, calf-roping and wrestling, wild-cow milking and the world-famous Royal Canadian Mounted Police Musical Wagon Ride. Overleaf a view of Calgary city center.

On winter weekends, Banff serves up to 10,000 skiers, mostly from Calgary, 80 miles to the east. A gondola, five chairlifts and three T-bars operate on 8,900-foot Sunshine Mountain and the facilities at Lake Louise can accommodate 7,000 skiers an hour. Seven thousand foot high Mount Norquay offers a stunning view of Banff and the Bow Valley and one of its runs, Lone Pine, is a steep 38°. The downhillers have been joined in recent years by converts to the fast growing cross-country skiing phenomenon.

The most pleasurable drive in all Alberta starts a few miles north of Banff. Motorists usually stop at mile-high, turquoise-hued Lake Louise before heading up the Icefields Parkway, a 140-mile-long highway that twists through stunning scenery on its way to Jasper.

Hugging mountain ridges and deep, green valleys, the parkway passes numerous snow-topped peaks and glaciers but none of the sights is quite as inspiring as the Columbia Icefields. Covering 300 square miles, the Columbia's three glaciers, Athabasca, Dome and Stutfield, are visible from the road: snowmobile tours take over 100,000 people every summer onto the Athabasca Glacier, where they can get out and walk on an ice-bed 1,000 feet thick.

With a population of around 3,000, Jasper is half the size of Banff. And although it isn't as big a tourist mecca either, it does run a respectable second to its sister town with two million annual visitors. Named after local trapper Jasper Hewes and located in the middle of a 4,200-square-mile national park, the town provides outlets for hiking, trail-riding, boating and skiing.

Unlike Banff, it doesn't have a world-renowned hot springs near the center of town but it does have the warmest mineral-water bath in the Rockies, 40 miles east at Miette. There's also a spectacular gorge and pleasant tearoom at Maligne Canyon, eight miles north of Jasper.

One of the half dozen lakes close to the town, Medicine Lake, has a subterranean drainage system that causes the water level to fluctuate from season to season. Believing that spirits controlled the changes, early Indians refused to go near the lake unless accompanied by a medicine man.

Edmonton

If there is one story Edmontonians like to tell more than others, it is the saga of Joe Shoctor. The son of an immigrant junk dealer, he was the sparkplug behind the launching of Alberta's first professional theater, the Citadel, in an old Salvation Army hall in 1965. Through hard toil and clever planning, Shoctor steered the Citadel to an impressive string of box-office hits: five years ago, the Citadel moved into a $6 million brick and glass showplace built on the same patch of ground where Shoctor's father had operated an open-air stall.

The Shoctor legend is more than just another local-boy-makes-good story. It has added meaning in Edmonton because his successful rise parallels, and thus gives physical embodiment to, the city's own development into a pulsing metropolis. Spawned by the emerging oil boom, skyscrapers began punching the downtown skyline in the 1960s while new subdivisions burst over the surrounding plains. Since 1966, the city population has gone from 370,000 to its present 521,200.

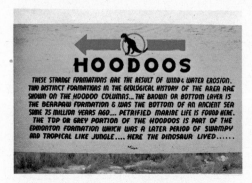

Dinosaur Provincial Park right and facing page top *is famous for its spectacular badland scenery and its dinosaur quarries and displays. Writing-on-Stone Provincial Park* facing page below *lies in the short-grass prairie region of Alberta, and was named after the Indian rock carvings and paintings which were found on the massive sandstone outcrops. The wind-and-rain sculpted rocks or hoodoos referred to in the notice* above *provide an other-worldly atmosphere. Hoodoos is the local name given to the strange upright columns of stone* these pages *and* overleaf *that are such a feature of the two Provincial parks.*

The sixties also introduced a curious celebration called Klondike Days to the provincial capital. For ten days every July, Edmontonians don brocade dresses, top hats and other Gay Nineties attire to attend Yukon-style dance halls, gold-panning competitions and raft-races. No one seems to be overly troubled by the reality that the K-Days fete is strangely misplaced; the Klondike Gold Rush took place 1,600 miles away. Indeed, the K-Days bash has grown from a local aberration drawing a few thousand participants in 1963 to a tourism bonanza, luring one million people a year.

History of an unquestionably authentic nature can be readily found throughout the city. The Ukrainian Museum displays embroidered costumes, wood carvings and household articles and the Provincial Museum devotes two separate galleries to dinosaur remains and items owned by pioneer farmers. Over on the South Shore, occupying a peaceful woodland at the edge of the North Saskatchewan River, sits Fort Edmonton. Completed in 1974, the fort's 20-foot high log gates open onto buildings and catwalks diligently crafted using original 19th-century tools. There's a blacksmith's shop, an outdoor baking oven and a re-creation of the quarters that belonged to the Hudson's Bay factor who established the post in 1846.

The fur-trading days are long gone but Edmonton is still something of a frontier town. Stores sell rifles and saddles, semis haul pipes and modular houses onto highways, young couples buy pickups and four-wheel-drives.

The frontier element is nicely balanced by a thriving cultural scene. Besides the Citadel Theater, Edmonton possesses an opera, a ballet, a dozen art galleries and a first-rate annual jazz festival. Pickup trucks and jeans proliferate on the main thoroughfare, Jasper Avenue, but a lot of people also drive Mercedes and Jaguars and wear New York fashions.

Calgary

The bronc-busters, rustlers and drifting gamblers and assorted characters who came to the southern Alberta grasslands 100 years ago have left Calgary an enviable legacy. Whereas many North American cities with populations in the same 590,000 range are bland carbon copies of one another, Calgary is thoroughly and delightfully immersed in a unique, Old West image. Businessmen wear hand-tooled cowboy boots, art galleries report a great demand for sculptures and oils featuring herd-riding cowhands, Nashville guitars twang incessantly on local airwaves.

Given this overtly Western atmosphere, it is perfectly logical that Calgarians refer to their cherished home as Cowtown. It makes good sense, too, that the biggest, brashest civic event of this or any other year, the Stampede, is a ten-day tribute to local cowboys, past and present. Steer wrestling, calf-roping and chuckwagon racing blend with square dances, casinos, pancake

The scenic grandeur of Alberta's Rocky Mountains is, without doubt, the great tourist attraction of the Province. Thousands of people every year visit Jasper National Park left and overleaf to holiday amongst the mountains.

33

breakfasts and – a concession to modern ways – a Disco Boogie Barn. Men and women strut about in Stetsons and high-heeled boots and some of the one million tourists succeed in looking even more Western than the locals, though they may come from Honolulu or Liverpool.

The city's Old West heritage is well represented at the Glenbow-Alberta Institute, a gleaming, $12 million museum that owes its existence to a modest, quiet-living Calgary lawyer who happened to be one of the wealthiest men in Canada. Eric Harvie amassed over $100 million when oil was discovered on land he'd bought in the 1940s for $10,000. He drove an old-model Studebaker and resided in the same unassuming house for 20 years. Yet when it came to his passion, collecting memorabilia, he spent lavishly.

Opened in 1976, the eight-story Glenbow has amongst its 125,000 books, paintings, artifacts and photographs, an outstanding collection of 1880s Indian and cowboy relics. Other items are, to say the least, varied. Queen Victoria's bloomers, Viscount Wolseley's swords and the Duke of Bedford's birds' eggs share space with African tribal masks and 30 pieces of Japanese armor. Before his death in 1975, Harvie donated the collection and $5 million to a provincial government fund that ensures the Glenbow's continued growth.

The Glenbow isn't the only visual symbol of the city's post-war blossoming. With 300 petroleum companies choosing Calgary for their headquarters (a decision, locals say, that can be attributed to the frequent mid-winter warm spells, the Chinooks, that Edmonton rarely experiences), the downtown area has undergone a development blitz. In 1977 alone Calgary issued $820 million in building permits, compared to Edmonton's $629 million. Amidst the glass and concrete towers, a few landmarks survive, notably the white, arcaded Bay building, the British lions perched on the Center Street bridge and the sedate, 68-year-old Palliser Hotel.

Not only do Calgarians put up more skyscrapers than Edmontonians but they tend to exhibit their wealth more zestfully too. There are more hot-tubs and swimming pools, more minks and limos, and more talk of weekend trips to Las Vegas on private jets. One mid-town shop offers its affluent customers $3,800 bathtubs equipped with gold faucets.

Most residents, however, must content themselves with much less expensive leisure activities. Fortunately, Calgary has a wide choice for them. In addition to year-round sporting and cultural events, the city has a 2.5-acre indoor park with 16,000 sub-tropical plants and a 66-acre historical park containing, among its 90 displays, a recreated 19th-century town. And then there's the cattle country. A short drive outside the city yields a visual treat: hundreds of miles of rollercoaster terrain occupied by sprawling ranches that, in some cases, are directly descended from spreads established by the province's first white settlers.

Of all the lakes to be found in Jasper National Park, Medicine Lake left *and* overleaf *is surely the most mysterious and romantic. Most of the year there is only a dry gravel bed here, but each spring meltwater from high in the mountains fills the lake to a depth of thirty feet. Then during the summer the water seeps away through the gravel, as if by magic, until there is only the dry lake bed left again.*

Of the many different species of wildlife inhabiting the Rockies these pages, the mountain goats and bighorn sheep favor the high alpine areas, and elk and deer prefer the lush forest meadows. Chipmunks, ground-squirrels and coyotes are not so particular about where they feed.

Banff National Park, comprising 2,564 square miles of peaks and glaciers, alpine meadows, forested slopes, rivers and lakes, is a wildlife paradise. The park's museum introduces the visitor to its many birds and animals which include beaver, muskrat, elk, mule deer, bighorn sheep and moose.

The Badlands

Seventy million years ago, a shallow, inland sea covered most of central and southern Alberta. Dinosaurs, crocodiles and flying reptiles inhabited humid swamps and forested hills rimming the great body of water. When the sea eventually receded, a valley filled with strangely-shaped sandstone and clay formations appeared on the banks of the Red Deer River: those bizarre, fossil-laden formations now entice 70,000 visitors every summer to Dinosaur Provincial Park, 140 miles east of Calgary.

Better known by their unofficial name, the Badlands, the bone-bearing grounds actually begin 80 miles west of the park gates near Drumheller, a community of 6,300 where a $27 million paleontological museum will open its doors in 1985. The muddy Red Deer curls past Drumheller and through a fossil-rich canyon into the park; the approach by road entails a 25-mile drive north from the farming center of Brooks; the blacktop ends abruptly at Lookout Point, a prairie-level spot where visitors can peer down and across the 25-mile-long valley.

This is, by far, the most unusual park in the country. Its stark, prehistoric topography and abundant dinosaur specimen beds persuaded UNESCO to declare it a World Heritage Site in 1979. The designation means that Dinosaur Provincial Park is protected under the same UN pact that applies to 56 other global locales – Mt. Everest National Park and the Florida Everglades among them.

Because of the necessity to preserve the valley, park wardens keep a tight rein on tourists. After driving down into the bowl from Lookout Point, they are asked to leave their vehicles at a campground and enter the park on supervised hikes or guided bus tours. Ninety per cent of the area is totally off-limits, except to a handful of licenced scientific teams searching for dinosaur remains

"There are hundreds of specimens lying on the surface or sticking partially out of the ground," says Philip Currie, an Alberta paleontologist who has spent the last four summers digging in the region. "If tourists were permitted to wander freely, someone might walk off with a bone belonging to a species we've never come across before."

Scientists started taking dinosaur remains out of the Badlands in 1889 but it wasn't until 1911 that a large-scale expedition was mounted. That was the year Barnum Brown, a paleontologist attached to the American Museum of Natural History, shipped a train-car load of bones to the New York institution. When it learned that Brown's finds included a new duck-billed species, the Geological Survey of Canada became alarmed at the prospect of losing more precious skeletons to a foreign museum: it promptly hired Charles Sternberg to lead this country's first major excavation mission in 1912. Since then, 400 skeletons or partial skeletons from 30 different species have been discovered in the Badlands.

The animals of the Rocky Mountains these pages are a fascinating mixture of prairie, forest, and arctic creatures. Each has its own environmental requirements and can only survive where these exist. The buffalo overleaf, once so numerous, now survive in special reserves.

By studying the bones and the places where they are found, paleontologists hope some day to unravel the riddle of what destroyed the beasts 65 million years ago. Theories range from a cosmic explosion to a global heat wave.

The park wardens' diligent efforts to protect the region will ultimately prove to be useless. Within the next 10,000 years, wind and rain is expected to erode the soft formations and turn Dinosaur Provincial Park into just another flat, barren, Prairie canyon.

The South

Although they may not be as freakishly-unique as the Badlands – or possess the Rockies' awesome grandeur – the Cypress Hills in the province's south east corner are a lovely, fascinating rarity. The hills cover 78 square miles and spill over the border into neighboring Saskatchewan; cacti, orchids and other sub-tropical plants pock the grassy slopes; evergreens crowd together in isolated coulees.

The sparkling waterfalls above make up part of the Athabasca Falls found in Jasper National Park in the Rocky Mountains. In the background can be seen Fryatt Mountain, which reaches a height of 11,026 feet. Two views of the Athabasca River can be seen right and above right, while facing page is a shimmering view of the Columbia Icefield. Jasper National Park, established in 1907, was named after Jasper House, a trading post set up by Jasper Hawes of the North West Company. The passes and valleys of the park were, however, explored long before 1907 – first by the fur traders, then by the railroad surveyors, geologists, botanists and mountaineers. Today there are more than 600 miles of hiking trails leading down through tranquil valleys, past deep blue lakes and up to remote, wind-swept ridges of high land. Besides hiking, favorite pastimes in this lovely park are fishing and photography. Overleaf and following pages show views of the Columbia Icefields.

Banff National Park these pages began as a 10-square-mile preserve around the Sulphur Mountain hot springs near the town of Banff. Since then the park, still famous for its springs, has grown to cover a staggering 2,564 square miles. Banff is Canada's oldest national park, established in 1885. It is a well-known skiing center, and canoeing and horseback riding are other popular activities. Hikers have a wide range of trails to choose from, each of which follows a path through spectacularly lovely and varied countryside. While Sunwapta Pass has become a major transport route far left, Lake Louise below is still a quiet, peaceful spot. This beautiful lake remained unknown until it was discovered by a railroad workman in 1882. Overleaf can be seen Moraine Lake in the Valley of the Ten Peaks.

Rising 5,000 feet above the surrounding plains, the Cypress Hills were, by virtue of a quirk of nature, almost untouched when the Ice Age froze the rest of Alberta 20,000 years ago. Indians once balked at entering the area, claiming it was the domain of the spirits that created thunderstorms. By the mid-1800s, local tribes were hunting, camping and, every now and then, battling each other there. Oddly enough, the most feared Indian leader to ever stay in the region refrained from fighting his enemies. Sitting Bull and 6,000 braves fled Wyoming following the Little Bighorn Massacre and established a camp in the Cypress Hills. A NWMP officer, James Walsh, finally convinced the Sioux chief after four years of negotiations to return to the United States.

Fifty miles north of the Cypress Hills stands the city of Medicine Hat. This community of 40,000 lists first-class glass and pottery factories amongst its assets. It is best known, however, for having an enormous natural-gas field beneath it. Drilling for water in 1883, a CPR crew struck one of the world's largest gas deposits: Medicine Hat residents now receive low-cost fuel from the city-owned source. On a Prairie tour, Rudyard Kipling dubbed the Hat, "the city with all hell for a basement."

Lethbridge has never had a huge gas field at its disposal but it was a thriving coal-mining center until the 1950s. Today, the city's 54,000 citizens are pleased to have Nikka Yuko, Canada's biggest Japanese garden, to show visitors: 3.7 acres of rocks, ponds, shrubs and Oriental buildings are presided over by girls in Japanese costume. Lethbridge was built on the site of the notorious Fort Whoop-Up, a fact that is remembered annually during a rodeo and fair bearing the title Whoop-Up Days.

Thirty miles west, a reconstructed stockade and museum sits on the edge of Oldman River at Fort Macleod. This is the spot where the NWMP erected their first post and, in honor of those trail-blazing lawmen, the mounted guards wear white helmets, red jackets and other 1880s gear.

The smallest national park in the Rockies, Waterton,

It was the magnificent scenery contained within its boundaries which earned Banff the distinction of being Canada's first national park.

Above *can be seen Altrude Lakes and left Big Beehive which both lie in the park. Mount Rundle previous pages is near the town of Banff itself.*

is an hour's drive west of Fort Macleod. The 200-square-mile park may be short on space but it contains the same mixture of lakes, mountain trails, glaciers and wildlife that exist in Banff and Jasper. Built in the 1920s, the log-hewn Prince of Wales Hotel provides a distinctive service for its guests: live chamber music during evening meals. The park itself is the Canadian section of the Waterton-Glacier International Peace Park.

The still, calm waters of First Vermilion Lake, and the little boats moored to the jetty opposite page, are a positive invitation to anyone wishing to get away from it all.
Moraine Lake below left, also situated in Banff National Park, opens the gateway to the Canadian Rockies from the west. *Banff Golf Course below proves an irresistible temptation to golfers from all over the world.* Peyto Lake *overleaf on the other hand is a center for anyone interested in hiking; the lake is named after a popular turn of the century local.*

The North

On a bitterly cold January night in 1929, 10,000 people turned out at an Edmonton airstrip to greet two men who had, to quote a local newspaper, "raced against death in the north." Wop May and Vic Horner had flown 600 miles in an open-cockpit biplane to deliver emergency drugs during a diphtheria epidemic. Wrapped in heavy coats, their goggles frosted, the pair had battled a snowstorm and a −30°F. temperature in a wood and cloth Avro Avian that wasn't even equipped with landing skis.

The May-Horner mercy flight was front-page news yet it was only one of many daring trips made by the pioneering bush pilots who helped open the northland to modern-day development. Starting in 1920, men like Punch Dickens, Grant McConachie and Archie McMillan flew prospectors, supplies and mail into remote settlements such as Fort Vermilion and Fort Chipewyan. On return trips, they carried furs, the sick and injured and, more than once, bush-weary trappers who drank homebrew all the way to Edmonton.

Fur trading, farming and logging were the economic mainstays of the vast, thickly-treed north until the 1950s. That's when a growing demand for petroleum prompted geological teams to investigate oil and gas deposits that explorers and prospectors had long known about. The massive Athabasca Tar Sands near Fort McMurray were, in fact, discovered by Peter Pond in 1778 and an enterprising Edmontonian, Sidney Ellis, had taken 60 tons of oil-soaked sand out by horse and wagon in 1915 to pave the city's streets.

A few ill-fated attempts to extract the oil from the sand occurred in the fifties. Then the Great Canadian Oil Sands Limited came up with a process in 1963 whereby the tar sand is strip-mined and the oil separated from it by a hot-water method. The process can't recover all of the estimated 600 billion barrels under the earth but experts feel enough can be extracted to make the Tar Sands a world leader.

At Peace River, 420 miles west of Fort McMurray, the talk is more likely to center on sport-fishing than oil. The Arctic grayling, pike and trout are so abundant that there is no closed season. Outside the town of Peace River, on a hill overlooking a river valley, lies the grave of Twelve-Foot Davis, a prospector who staked a claim on a 12-foot patch between two bigger tracts and found $15,000 worth of gold. The large statue of Davis at the gravesite is a strong reminder that Peace River citizens, like other Albertans, are immensely proud of their historical heritage.

Farming is one of Alberta's richest industries. The first attempt at cultivating the province's soil was back in 1779, when a certain Peter Pond planted a small garden near Lake Athabasca. This picture facing page top gives an idea of the progress of agriculture since then! Ponoka facing page below left lies on Alberta Number 2 highway, which passes the rapeseed fields of Fairview top left and through the farmlands around Beaverlodge left.

The Annual "Touring Tin" rally from Calgary to Banff

First published 1983 by
  Collins Publishers, 100 Lesmill Road, Don Mills, Ontario.
© 1983 Text: Collins Publishers
© 1983 Photography: Colour Library Books Ltd.,
  Guildford, Surrey, England.
Colour separations by Fercrom
Display and text filmsetting by Acesetters Ltd.,
  Richmond, Surrey, England.
Printed and bound in Barcelona, Spain, by I. G. DOMINGO
  and Eurobinder

Canadian Cataloguing in Publication Data.
Ferguson, Ted.
   Alberta a symphony in color
ISBN 0-00-217031-0
1. Alberta - Description and travel - 1950   - Views.*
I. Title.
FC3667.3.F37   917.123'043'0222   C83-098643-X
F1076.F37